Witness Report

poems by

Roger W. Hecht

Finishing Line Press
Georgetown, Kentucky

Witness Report

Copyright © 2020 by Roger W. Hecht
ISBN 978-1-64662-180-4 First Edition
All rights reserved under International and Pan-American Copyright Conventions. No part of this book may be reproduced in any manner whatsoever without written permission from the publisher, except in the case of brief quotations embodied in critical articles and reviews.

ACKNOWLEDGMENTS

I would like to express my endless gratitude for the support I've received from my colleagues and especially from my family. Many thanks, too, to the editors of the following publications where these poems first made their appearance.

Bracken: "Villanelle"
Diaphanous Journal of Literary and Visual Art: "Dharma," "Sad Miracle"
From the Finger Lakes: A Poetry Anthology (Ithaca, Cayuga Lakes Books): "Sky Burial," "Witness Report"
Like Light: 25 Years of Poetry & Prose by Bright Hill Poets & Writers: "And on this day…"
The Otter: "Sky Burial"
Prick of the Spindle: Prose Poem ("I am the bones of the boy")
Sheila-Na-Gig: "Shoe Town, 1980"
Shortest Day; Longest Night: Stories and Poems from the Solstice Shorts Festival (London: Arachne Press): "The Ornery Orrery"
The Basil O'Flaherty: "Like Scissors," "Signs"
Yes, Poetry: "Sunlight Beckons Beyond the Dumpster"

Publisher: Leah Maines
Editor: Christen Kincaid
Cover Art: Iwase Takanori, *River Crow*
Author Photo: Joan Marcus
Cover Design: Elizabeth Maines McCleavy

Printed in the USA on acid-free paper.
Order online: www.finishinglinepress.com
also available on amazon.com

Author inquiries and mail orders:
Finishing Line Press
P. O. Box 1626
Georgetown, Kentucky 40324
U. S. A.

Table of Contents

Witness Report 1

Villanelle 3

And on this day… 4

Prose Poem 7

The Ornery Orrery 8

Sunlight Beckons Beyond the Dumpster 9

Blue Mug 11

Shoe Town, 1980 12

473 mph 14

eat & be eaten 15

Sad Miracle 16

For Emily 17

No Church 18

Signs 20

Like Scissors 21

Dharma 22

Sky Burial 24

This book is for Joan

Witness Report

You couldn't tell distress
in the duck's face, not from
the distance we watched it.

Maybe in her gait, or in the rapid
turns of her head with the
traffic whizzing past. Certainly,

the raft of ducklings strung in a line
then rushing in behind her
showed, at the very least, confusion.

The duck hopped a granite curb
the ducklings couldn't leap.
It seemed a storybook tragedy

was playing out before us. A man
tried herding them to the sidewalk,
waving off cars that slowed

& fortunately didn't wreck.
& when the ducks turned back
across the road, we knew

the resulting mess would form the stories
the dozen of us watching
helplessly from the gas station pumps

might tell our friends that night
at dinner or over drinks.
We're a sentimental town.

But all the lights were with them.
A woman lifted duckling after duckling
from the blacktop to the grass,

where the duck & brood regrouped
& could safely wander
to their certain deaths

sometime off in the future. & so
one by one we all drive off
with a great appreciation

of just what kind of world we have made.

Villanelle

The sun sinks past the great beyond,
or at least beyond the horizon,
& sets aflame the skin of Jenning's Pond,

a red & molten blue reflection
stirred only by the misstep of a heron.
The sun sinks, & beyond

deep in the trees, young
coyotes hunker till their midnight song
sets aflame the skin of Jenning's Pond

& tears my ears toward that direction
our cat unwittingly wandered
into teeth & terror and the great beyond

that summer night. Their meal our grief, and so on.
The trees turned their heads; now their leaves turn on
& set aflame the skin of Jenning's Pond,

a red & yellow & rust pointillist explosion
that draws us to the jaws of their oblivion—
our joy & delight till the sun sinks. The great beyond.
& all aflame the skin of Jenning's Pond.

And on this day...

I will write a poem Garrison Keillor
could read on the radio. Each word
formed around the sound of his voice,

lines & pauses aligned to the measure
of his Minnesota breath.
& let there be S's enough

so the whistles through his teeth
mirror the wind in the trees
where the poem goes:

a cabin by a lake in the Adirondacks perhaps,
or the West Virginia hills where your family
failed repeatedly to build

that summer house—
weekends hacking hopelessly at undergrowth
that regenerated into impenetrable walls

leaving you with only
the vague warmth of a flimsy campfire,
hotdogs & tea & a dirty flannel shirt,

the kind Keillor might sport
on Minnesota mornings chopping firewood
or writing scripts—till your parents

gave up & bought a condo at the beach.
But that doesn't matter, because Keillor's
warm accent & the soft

Americana piano chords envelop you in
nostalgia enough to remind you how
you don't live there, never did,

& where ever you do live
—a ranch or colonial
spotting a cul-de-sac somewhere,

or a cramped city walk-up where
street lights and sirens
fill the windows all night—

is a place to escape,
a place to seek refuge,
there among the maples & pines & small stands of birch,

the leaf and needle-strewn shoreline,
the lake's rippled surface reflecting and distorting
a darkening sky—too cold to swim now—

so you listen to the night settling in,
the birds settling down, not too many insects,
not much sunlight left,

so you wait for evening's last spotlight
to pierce the branches & the kitchen window
lined with bottles a century old

dug from old trash heaps half a century ago
when you were the sort of exploring boy
you always thought you would be,

easing them from the mud, rinsing them in a creek,
saving only the best: bottles with colors
they don't make anymore

once filled with mysterious potions
they don't make anymore,
& the marmalade sunlight filling the kitchen

with upended bottle-light rainbows
makes the cabin a homespun Chartres
filled with promise & youth you promised yourself

you would always cling to.
That's how you remember it,
or how you would remember it

if you ever had a cabin, or a cabin that wasn't
just a poem in the voice of Garrison Keillor
whistling and whispering through the radio

mixing with the fade-in of Americana piano
which tinkles to a stop.
Then news from the latest war.

Prose Poem

I am the bones of the boy buried in the cellar. The boy the cellar was built for. The boy that was here long before there were cellars. I am the bones of the boy, but I am not the boy. I am the bones of the boy in a congress of bones, a body of boys long gone, a body that meets when there is nothing to say & no way to say it & cannot sleep. The bones of the mice the bones of the cats dragged in scramble the rafters to invisible nests. Their sinews dissolved, they motion back to dust where they sleep, reassemble & scramble, a different mouse each night. I never sleep, being bones still clinging to their boyhood. The boys call their meetings to order, slap secret handshakes, throw hand signs & fingers into far corners. Each meeting each presiding officer resigns until the body finally dissolves. Again & again the motion dies. Then the boys in the bones will be no longer present to say *here*. Let's say the boys lit out for the frontier where there is no grass to trip them up, no roots to tangle their feet, the way they entangled me. Roots worm into the cellar. Worms root our demise. The boys who once hooked them for fish bait are now meals in the fields where circling birds remind them of universal forms stacked like legos, logos, the law they could never avoid.

The boys unhinge their jaws as if they could be heard. They have no use for words now, no use for limbs. No use for the hands that held them down.

The Ornery Orrery

"Egad!" cried Machiavelli. "This orrery is stuck! The planets don't align. Now, how will I predict the rise & fall of kings, the comings & goings of plagues, & on which horse God wills me to place my ducats?" Leonardo, with an eye toward the mechanical, squinted at the marvelous machine: its wheels & gorgeously engraved discs, its metal spheres perched on sticks. He tried its brass gears, tightened & loosened screws, worried the crank. He recognized the problem at once. "Fool," he cried, popping the flat-topped cap off the Florentine's head. "Don't you see? This machine can't even exist! We live in a geocentric universe. This heliocentric universe won't be confirmed for a hundred & fifty years!" He re-labeled the celestial objects & the truth came perfectly clear. "Besides, your dripping candle jammed it here." He flicked a plug of wax off with his knife, turned the crank, & set the future in motion. The wheels turned freely. Planets spun their orbits. Eclipses came & went. Fruits tumbled from their branches. Princes became obsolete while the sun stayed firmly in place. "I see," the master statesman murmured, astounded, as his world fell to ruins before his eyes like clockwork.

Sunlight Beckons Beyond the Dumpster

My twelve-year-old daughter, reading a novel,
comes across a new word. She asks, "what is *dauntless*?"
I say, "To lack daunt. To be without it." As if that helps.
She asks, "So, do we have any?" I have to say I don't know.
No one ever asked. & I wouldn't know where to look.
The bookshelf? The back of the fridge? Nothing.
So next time I'm downtown and some worn out guy
stretches out a hand I'll have to shrug, point to my hips
& make the empty-pocket gesture & say with my face,
maybe next time, bro; because you see, I'm dauntless.
& I'd walk away embarrassed because maybe that's a lie
& I have some beside the quarters in my car's cup holder
that I didn't give to the guy with the sign on the corner
near Dunkin Donuts when I stopped at the light.
Or not. Because probably really I'm dauntless. Which is not
to say I'm undaunted, since that presumes I once had it,
or having lost it plan to get some more. Getting some,
what would I do with it? What would anyone do?
Invest it, I guess. But not in a bank; not at these rates.
I'd have to find a firm. Invest aggressively. Take risks.
Watch my daunt grow. Buy up companies; sell off the parts.
Get it at the source: mines, mineral rights, key lanes of transport.
Workers toiling night & day: mountain tops removed; slick water
horizontal drill rigs churning; whole forests leveled & replanted
to monocrop daunt. Because there's only so much of it
& so much need, & if there isn't need I'll make it with ads
on the Sunday morning talk shows & Buzzfeed pop-ups.
So long as I can keep the unions out. Easy enough
if I spread some around the right people. But really,
I'm not that ambitious & don't think myself greedy.
I just want enough for me. How I get it doesn't matter.
Let's just say I met a guy who knows a guy who has a connection
& told me when to meet him in the alley behind the Shoremart.
Yes, it costs more than I want, but I don't get to set the price.
I meet the man, who offers me a taste, because that's good business.
I can feel my cheeks flush & that pleasant buzzing on my gums.

But around the block there's another two guys waiting,
which I should have expected. I don't resist, but I don't show fear.
My impulse is to stare at the gun, but I look the guy
right in the eye. He's scared too & refuses my gaze. His partner
rifles my pockets, shoves me hard against the dumpster.
I hold my own: chest out, heart racing, on the verge of tears.
It's snowing maybe, or raining, or maybe the sun is out
& a warm breeze is telling me to pull myself out of the shadows
& start the day on a firmer foot. But I remain on the greasy bricks
stuck in darkness where I am: fearful & needy
& full of remorse, undaunted & still dauntless.

Blue Mug

That big blue mug
with the bowed out sides
pregnant with warmth

filling your palm while
fingers and the knuckles
gripping the ceramic loop

produce the illusion you can
handle anything—
it's no good,

or not as good as it seemed
at the store. It seemed generous.
It gives too much:

too much hot drink, too much soup,
more than you can manage.
It places demands

you can never meet, that you finish
what you start at the pace it sets,
the rate it dissipates heat,

so by the time you find
the perfect sip the coffee's cold
& the mug's only just half empty.

Re-heating in the microwave
is not an inconvenience,
it's a sad admission.

To be disappointed in the mug is displaced.
The mug knows better.
The disappointment is you.

Shoe Town, 1980

Straightening women's shoes in the size 8 aisle.
I'm only sixteen. It's my first real job.
I find strays on the benches, never their mates.
I shadow two black women in their thirties.

I'm only sixteen. It's my first real job.
I watch heat rise off the parking lot through the glass double doors
& shadow two black women in their thirties.
One seems done with work; the other fresh off the tennis court.

I watch heat rise off the parking lot through the glass double doors,
No one seems to know what they're looking for.
One seems done with work; the other fresh off the tennis court.
The manager in the storeroom crouches behind boxes.

No one seems to know what they're looking for.
I ask, *is there something in particular you want?*
The manager in the storeroom crouches behind the boxes
Looking through a one-way glass.

I ask, *is there something in particular you want?*
I want them to think I'm being helpful.
Looking through a one-way glass
Not fully comprehending what I see.

I want them to think I'm being helpful.
I work with a kid with an artificial eye
Not fully comprehending what I see.
He said with a straight face he didn't like niggers.

I work with a kid with an artificial eye
who always came back from break smelling of smoke.
He said with a straight face he didn't like niggers.
Just like the manager. On the floor, he always smiles.

He always came back from break smelling of smoke.
I get yelled at when my own break runs too long.
Just like the manager, on the floor, he always smiles,
& helps her find the blue pump she wants.

I get yelled at when my own break runs too long,
& make up my mind to quit, but not before
I help her find the blue pump she wants,
still pretending I'm shadowing them.

I make up my mind to quit, but not before
straightening shoes in the size 8 aisle,
still pretending. I'm shadowing them.
I find strays on the benches. Never their mates.

473 mph

A little blue plane
sits atop Montana.
What's it doing there?

A little blue plane
astraddle a map,
wingtip touching a river.

You wouldn't know
it's moving but for
the red line it drags

across the states.
The boat in the harbor
still among the ripples,

the way a comet hangs
still among the stars—
trailing white lines

give away motion.
White noise & gentle sway,
the clouds creep

along with us.
The wonder of it,
the speed that keeps us

at this stillness
screaming
at 35,000 feet above.

Below, we silently crawl
at an ant's pace
to anyone caring to look.

eat & be eaten

is not a choice   no
malice   no ill
will   only appetite—
the krill   the whale
yours   mine   what-
ever hunger lingers
behind that tree or
under the mud
so by all means
raise your empire
watch it crumble
make your money
be kind   cruelty
hinders no one else's
hunger   find beauty in
a corpse   a copse
of maples dropping
leaves by the handful
on the surface of
a lake   the swell of
a breast   curve of
an ass   drunk
off another's passion
get lost in the depths
of flesh   eat heartily
by all means have
lots of kids to love
to feed & later to be
fed to the silent waves
of bacteria   to the
larval fly

Sad Miracle

That anything's alive is miraculous
though I don't believe in miracles. But outside
the minus-five cold encases the trees,
stiffens snow. Still, new tracks bisect the field,
a woodpecker batters a frozen stump,
& there's a cabbage white butterfly
glued to the window above the sink,
waiting out the naked maples
in the heatless light of a compact florescent bulb.

On what harvest did it hitch a ride to my kitchen,
& how will I keep it alive?

Days pass. It bypasses the plate of rotten cantaloupe
I try to pass off as nectar. The morning sun's
an ice ball. The trees refuse to flower.
Days pass indifferent. Flexing its white wings,
The butterfly dedicates itself to waiting…, for what?
Waiting out the clock. It's a miracle
of bad timing with nothing to pollinate
& no metamorphosis
except into a relic on my shelf.

For Emily

I heard a girl die—when I buzzed
The window's still glass
Tremor'd as my beating failed
To catch the deaden'd breeze

Mourners multiplied—my compound eye
saw hundreds—leaning in
look up—tremble—parse their breath
the Day's last light grew thin

The girl accepted flowers, water
Handed hanks of hair
To whoever thanked her for them—
For me t'was nothing there

No wine, no cakes, no sugar, no tea
Just a black book's brim
I tried to flee—then She died
I sensed my meal then

No Church

I have known no church
that wasn't instead
a museum of grief:

frescoes, finger bones,
effigies of ancient saints
stapled with money, milagros

& pleas for relief
of some sort or other
received, or—

who knows what type
of relief is received
just from asking?

Who gives it? Who cares?
I was given
the pleasure of looking:

the meticulous work
of hands, of eyes turned
inward to visions gleaned

from everyday suffering
that seeks purpose
or at least an end,

suffering that still persists
but with a different cast
in a world of 24 hour endless light.

What did the carvers
of saints' faces, the painters
of mothers of martyrs

have that we lack
& so desperately need?
The necessary darkness

for a vision to arise
from the quivering glow
of candle stump or lamp

when the oil runs out.
The eyes then turn to
the only reliable

source of light—
dusk on the horizon,
or, later, the dawn.

Signs

The Romans read entrails to discern the future.
We read stools for signs: too much fiber,
cancer, foreclosure. The Jews force-fed maggots
to Roman goats
to buy themselves time in the dust of Masada.
We eat Kale & cabbage, açai
bowls sprinkled with chia seeds, determined
to extend our days another day. You'll find
us tending our gut flora with the acuity of termites
turning a forest to soil. & in the time
It's taken to tend these lines another species has died—
a fish, a frog, an insect—unseen by us, who've tried
so hard to interpret the signs of the world we made,
ignoring our spot in the extinction parade.

Like Scissors

Like scissors they snip
the chemical threads
that hold a live thing
together: bacteria,
fungus, primordial swarm.
Then we're gas. Then
we become element:
phosphorus, carbon,
something a live
plant can claim. Dead,
we're soup, we're cheese,
we're the meal we're
invited to but can never
enjoy. Enjoyed—
if a mold knows joy—
let's say sated on,
feted because we're feast,
the last supper we'll never
know because by then
we're already being
resurrected back into
the body of the world.

Dharma

I am I because a little worm bites me
I am I filled with I's and eyes watching what happens next

I am a host/I am inhabited
I am a whole world colonized
a body embodied, bodies burrowed in my pores,
    my hair, my lungs, my eyes
Whose bodies are borne forth when I strut?
Whose being breathes each deep sweet breath?
When I inhale whose lungs fill with air?
Do I walk, or am I conducted?
What DNA varies my mind when I turn on the TV?
When I sip a beer what yeast's thirst does my deep drink slake?

I am host/I am inhabited
I'm a whole ecosystem complete with theology
unraveled, the DNA thread more not me than me strung like a lyre,
let the wind strum sing my song
I sing the body organic
I sing the matter inside me
Am I its god going about my business, tending the infrastructure, nerves,
    veins, capillaries, pores
    conducting all beings to the spaces they visit:
domodex follicorum skitters on a follicle, doing its mite dance, setting its
    teeth in an old dried flake of skin
there's one now leaning on an eyelash, waiting for its mate in the
    blood-lit night
Lactobacillus soft blankets, smooth as new snow, churning its germs,
sweetening the milk I drink
Entero bacteriacoea, my probiotic protectors, beating back all that
    salmonella that would make me sick
h. pylori pissed off and mean,
    burning holes in my gut just for the fun it

I don't know what I am, or what to make of me now
Mitochondria shuffle the deck:
I'm a virus on the planet,
I am a planet for a mite, a forest of invisible fauna
      each with its claim on me
Cell lines, whole families
      speaking their chemical language, cultures,
           whole civilizations
I am Mahayana, greater vehicle
impacting a million lifetimes' karma each time I cough

Pediculus humanus captis, do you ever wonder what you are?
You turn your monstrous pin-point face
undaunted by any existential doubt
      & plunge unflinching your teeth deep into my dermis
           my blood belonging to me as good belongs to you

worms in my stomach
worms in my eye
worms in my brain
I contain multitudes
I'm giving up the ghost
I am a ghost hosting worm ghosts & all my relations
a dot in the universe expanding in space
Expanding & waiting to collide with
whatever come what may

See me expand. Watch me grow.
Big Bang.

Sky Burial

If only I could see
& smell, could
keep my senses
as I lose them
wouldn't I find it
delicious? The enzymes
without me replacing
the enzymes
within me replacing
cell by cell
my body. Such
transcendence! Patiently
they're waiting the day
my defenses
diminish, waiting
to transfigure.
& while I diminish
I will swell
like pride with gasses,
anticipating
my higher function:
protein for the cleansing
birds, a nest
my hair, my braincase
shelter for a mouse.
If I were any other
animal my skin
might become shoes,
my bones knives
or needles or buttons
or combs. It is fitting.
Nothing about me
wasted. Nothing
about me not becoming
something else.

Roger W. Hecht's books include a poetry collection, *Talking Pictures* (Cervena Barva Press) and a chapbook, *Lunch at the Table of Opposites* (Red Dancefloor Press). He is the editor of two works: *The Erie Canal Reader*, 1790-1950 (Syracuse University Press) and *Freemen Awake! Rally Songs and Poems from New York's Anti-Rent War* (Delaware Co. Historical Society). His poems have appeared widely in such venues as *Denver Quarterly, Diagram, Puerto del Sol, Sheila-na-gig, Bracken, The Piltdown Review* and many others. He has also published essays on James Fenimore Cooper, Herman Melville, and Harriett Beecher Stowe. In his poetry and his research, Hecht is interested in the intersection of the natural environment, art, and politics. He earned his B.A. in English from the University of Maryland, his M.F.A. in poetry from the University of Arizona, and his Ph.D. in English from Syracuse University. He is currently an Associate Professor of English at SUNY, Oneonta, where he helps direct the Red Dragon Reading Series, and is researching a book on the environmental themes in the films of the famed anime powerhouse, Studio Ghibli.

www.ingramcontent.com/pod-product-compliance
Lightning Source LLC
LaVergne TN
LVHW090039090426
835510LV00038B/967